THE
SPIRITUAL
MILLIONAIRE

THE
SPIRITUAL
MILLIONAIRE

The Spirit of Wisdom Will Make You Rich

KEITH CAMERON SMITH

WKU Publishing

Published by WKU Publishing
10 Eloise Circle
Ormond Beach, Florida 32176
Tel: 386-441-0028
www.keithcameronsmith.com

PUBLISHER'S CATALOGING-IN-PUBLICATION DATA
Smith, Keith Cameron.
   The spiritual millionaire : the spirit of wisdom will make you rich /
Keith Cameron Smith — Ormond Beach, FL : WKU Publishing,
2004.
   p. ; cm.
   ISBN 0-9755070-0-1

   1. Wealth—Religious aspects. 2. Wisdom—Religious aspects.
   3. Spiritual life. 4. Quality of life. I. Title.

BL65.W42 S65 2004   2004106706
204/.4—dc22   CIP

Printed in the United States of America

10 9 8 7 6 5 4 3 2 1

Edited by Mary Jo Zazueta
Cover and interior design by To The Point Solutions

The principles described in this book have made me rich in every area of my life. I know they will do the same for you—if you apply them.

CONTENTS

CONTENTS

THE
SPIRITUAL
MILLIONAIRE

INTRODUCTION

THIS BOOK IS ABOUT letting the Spirit of Wisdom expand your mind to become a millionaire in a spiritual way. The Spirit of Wisdom will show you how to create millions of dollars—if you learn to hear and heed Her instructions. Wisdom is the application of knowledge. There are proven ways of becoming a millionaire that are based on the knowledge of people. The ways that God will show you how to make millions are based on His knowledge.

The knowledge of people is limited, whereas the knowledge of God is unlimited. God is infinite. The Spirit of Wisdom has an infinite supply of ideas on how to become financially wealthy. When you know the Spirit of Wisdom, then you will learn ways to create fortunes that have not yet been discovered. The catch is: The Spirit of Wisdom won't show you how to make millions until you learn to think from a spiritual point of view.

Being wealthy means much more than just financial abundance. To be wealthy spiritually, emotionally, mentally, and physically is more important than financial wealth alone. Financial abundance doesn't mean much if your health is bad or if you don't have peace of mind or if you don't have meaningful relationships or if you don't feel close to our Creator. A Spiritual Millionaire is rich in every area of his life.

Many of today's millionaires attribute their financial success to the Spirit of Wisdom. If you listen, the Spirit of Wisdom will teach you how to become a Spiritual Millionaire, too. A Spiritual Millionaire accumulates riches through the benefits of spiritual ideas and practices.

God is the Spirit of Wisdom. I will use the words *God* and the *Spirit of Wisdom* interchangeably throughout this book. When I speak of God, I will say He. When I speak of the Spirit of Wisdom, I will say She. God is Spirit. He/She is neither male nor female, but has characteristics of each.

Thinking of God as having both male and female characteristics will give you a better understanding of our Creator. The Scriptures refer to the male and female sides of God. For example, the book of Proverbs refers to Wisdom as She and Jesus taught His disciples to pray the Our Father. If you get nothing else from this book, I hope you gain a deeper under-standing of God having both male and female charac-teristics; although I expect you'll get much more.

Each chapter begins with the same verses from Proverbs about the Spirit of Wisdom. This is inten-tional. Repetition is a great teacher. After a few chap-ters, you may be tempted to skip over these verses, but don't. These verses reinforce the benefits of Wisdom and are worth reading over and over again. In fact, I suggest you write them down and display them where you can read them daily.

Read *The Spiritual Millionaire* with an open mind and a humble heart. Listen for God to speak to your heart while you read. You may hear a new million-dollar idea or be reminded of one you already knew about. God wants to bless you with financial abundance, so you can use money to improve this world and enjoy your life. It is a blessing from God for a person to enjoy his/her time under the sun. It is a blessing from God to enjoy the fruits of your labor. Spiritual Millionaires enjoy creating wealth and then using their abundance for God's purposes.

Chapter One

THE SPIRIT OF WISDOM

Happy is the man who finds Wisdom and the man who gains understanding. For her proceeds are better than the profits of silver, and her gain better than fine gold. She is more precious than rubies and all the things you may desire cannot compare with her. Long life is in her right hand; in her left hand are riches and honor. Her ways are ways of pleasantness and all her paths are peace.

[Proverbs 3:13-17]

THE SPIRIT OF Wisdom wants to make you rich spiritually, emotionally, mentally, and physically before She makes you rich in finances. Proverbs says Her proceeds are better than the profits of silver and Her gain better than fine gold. What is better than money? One answer is relationships; meaningful relationships that enhance the quality of your life and bring you great joy and fulfillment.

Your spiritual life is about having a relationship with God. There is no greater joy or fulfillment than having a relationship with God. I am not talking about being religious and just having *knowledge* about God—but actually experiencing the Spirit of Wisdom in your daily life. There are many religious people in the world but few who are truly spiritual. Being spiritual is more than acquiring knowledge about God, it is actually *knowing* Him. Being spiritual is not about religious activity; it is about experiencing loving relationships. It is about loving God, people, and yourself.

The title of this book is not *The Religious Millionaire* because being religious will not make you rich—but being spiritual will. Religious people have knowledge about God, but not necessarily a real relationship with Him. Spiritual Millionaires have a relationship with the Spirit of Wisdom. Knowing *about* someone is different than actually knowing him or her. Having a relationship with God is better than having money or anything money can buy.

You are emotionally rich when you have meaningful relationships with people. Emotional riches are far greater than financial riches. The Spirit of Wisdom wants you to have meaningful relationships with people. There are millionaires in the world today who would gladly give up their money to have significant relationships.

Many people lose their families trying to obtain financial riches. Spiritual Millionaires have great family lives and many faithful friends. Money cannot compare to having a home full of love and a strong circle of friends. The Spiritual Millionaires' relationship with God empowers them to have deep, meaningful relationships with other people. They would not give up their loving relationships for all the money in the world. The Spirit of Wisdom teaches people how to become emotionally rich before She teaches them how to become financially rich.

Your mental and physical lives reflect how you treat yourself. Being mentally rich is having peace of mind. You can't put a price on piece of mind. Many millionaires who are not spiritual have enormous amounts of stress and worry. Some are concerned about losing their money and some have strained relationships with their family—and some experience both.

What good is money if you don't have peace of mind? The Spiritual Millionaire would rather be poor and have peace of mind than be monetarily wealthy and be stressed, worried, and fearful. Proverbs says of Wisdom, "all Her paths are peace."

Being physically rich is to be in good health. Proverbs says, "Long life is in Her right hand, and in Her left are riches and honor." There is the old saying that many people give their health away trying to get wealth and then would gladly give their wealth away to get their health back.

The Spiritual Millionaire is healthy and wealthy. Money won't mean much to you if your health is bad. The Spirit of Wisdom teaches you to be mentally and physically rich before she teaches you to be financially rich.

Being financially wealthy is a benefit of the Spirit of Wisdom. She wants you to have financial abundance, but not before She makes you rich in other areas of life. God wants you to be financially rich so you can use money to accomplish His purposes.

The Spirit of Wisdom teaches you to be rich in other areas of life first, because if She didn't you would use your money for only selfish reasons. Becoming rich in the other areas of your life will give you incredible joy. And when you experience the joy of being spiritually, emotionally, mentally, and physically rich, then you will want to use your money to help others become rich in every area of their lives. The Spiritual Millionaire wants to improve the quality of life for as many people as possible.

There is the Spirit of Wisdom and there is wisdom of the world. The book of James 3:13-18 discusses the differences between the wisdom of the world and the Spirit of Wisdom. It says, "Who is wise and understanding among you? Let him show by good conduct that his works are done in the meekness of wisdom. But if you have bitter envy and self-seeking in your hearts do not boast and lie against the truth. This wisdom does not descend from above but is earthly, sensual, demonic. For where envy and self-seeking exist, confusion and every evil thing are there. But the wisdom that is from above is first pure, then peaceable, gentle, willing to yield, full of mercy and good fruits, without partiality and without hypocrisy. Now the fruit of righteousness is sown in peace by those who make peace."

The Spirit of Wisdom is generous and brings peace into your life. The wisdom of the world is selfish and brings confusion into your life. You can become financially rich through selfishness, manipulation, intimidation, and other wicked ways; but it will fill your life with sorrow. Proverbs 10:22 says, "The blessing of the Lord makes one rich, and He adds no sorrow with it." The Spirit of Wisdom brings peace and joy into every area of your life and wants you to share that peace and joy with others. The wisdom of the world brings stress and depression into your life. If you do not know God personally, then the wisdom of the world is the only way you know how to live. Spiritual Millionaires have personal relationships with God and the Spirit of Wisdom shows them how to become rich in all areas of their lives.

The Spirit of Wisdom gives you the power to make the right choices. Wisdom is the ability to make the right decisions. Notice James 3 says, "If you are wise and understanding, then show it by your good conduct." Good conduct is right actions and right decisions. Right actions are the result of right thinking and speaking. Wisdom is the ability to think right thoughts, speak right words, and make right decisions. That which brings you peace is what is right.

Purpose is the path to peace. This is where knowing the Spirit of Wisdom comes in. Your Creator knows the purposes for which He created you. Your purposes are what are right for you. Spiritual Millionaires know their purposes and think about them constantly. Everyone has spiritual, emotional, mental, physical, and financial purposes. Fulfilling your purposes will bring you peace and prosperity.

Some of your purposes are for you alone. The unique purposes of your life are right for you. What is right for you may not be right for someone else. Listening to the Spirit of Wisdom keeps you focused on what is right for you. Listening to other people tell you what they think is right for you can distract you from your purposes and keep you from becoming rich.

The Spirit of Wisdom teaches you how to think, speak, and act in line with the things you were created to do. You were created to live by faith. Scriptures say, "The just shall live by faith." Spiritual Millionaires live by faith. They understand that Wisdom is the ability to make the right decisions and that living by faith is always the right decision. It takes faith to become rich; faith in God, people, and yourself. The Spirit of Wisdom teaches you how to overcome fear with faith and become rich in every area of your life.

Chapter Two

FAITH AND FEAR

Happy is the man who finds Wisdom and the man who gains understanding. For her proceeds are better than the profits of silver, and her gain better than fine gold. She is more precious than rubies and all the things you may desire cannot compare with her. Long life is in her right hand; in her left hand are riches and honor. Her ways are ways of pleasantness and all her paths are peace.

[Proverbs 3:13-17]

THE SPIRITUAL MILLIONAIRE has learned to overcome fear with faith. Faith cannot operate without hope for "Faith is the substance of things hoped for, the evidence of things unseen." [Hebrews 11:1] Hope shines in the Spiritual Millionaire's heart and mind.

True hope has no doubts. Faith cannot operate when you doubt. Doubt is the relative of fear. Fear is the substance of things doubted. Faith and fear both have the power to manifest things into your life. Whatever you have faith for, will come into your life. Whatever you fear will also come into your life.

The Spiritual Millionaire uses faith and hope to become rich. If you believe you can become a millionaire, that's hope. When you believe you will become a millionaire, that's faith. The Spiritual Millionaire believes they can and will become rich before they actually do. If you doubt that you can become a millionaire, then you won't. Doubt turns off the lights in your life. Many people are afraid of the dark because they can't see. Doubt opens the door to let fear enter your life. Financial fear is the result of not being able to see how you can make money. People can't see how to become millionaires because they doubt they can. Doubt is darkness. Hope is light. Hope is believing you can. When you believe you can, then you have light to see how to make money. Faith starts to work when you have hope.

The Spirit of Wisdom teaches you truth. Faith and hope come from believing truth. Fear and doubt come from believing lies. "You shall know the truth and the truth shall set you free." [John 8:32] Faith and hope bring freedom. Fear and doubt bring bondage. You shall believe a lie and the lie will put you into bondage. You shall know the truth about money and the truth about money will set you free financially.

One truth that a Spiritual Millionaire believes is that God wants him to be rich. This truth brings hope and the light from the hope brings faith to see how to become a millionaire. Faith acts on hope and accomplishes whatever it believes in. Faith is the right thought that produces the right action to manifest money.

In contrast, fear acts on doubt and brings the very thing that you are afraid of into your life. Fear is wrong thinking that produces wrong actions and brings wrong things into your life.

Wisdom is the application of knowledge. Knowledge is truth. The Spirit of Wisdom teaches you to believe and act on truth. Truth is spiritual light. Lies are darkness. If you do not believe that God wants you to be rich then you believe a lie. That lie will keep you in darkness and the darkness will keep you from being able to see how to become rich. Any lie in any area of your life will keep you from being rich in that area. Lies about God keep you from spiritual riches. Lies about people keep you from emotional riches. Lies about yourself keep you from mental riches. Lies about health keep you from physical riches. And lies about money keep you from financial riches.

The truth in any area of life makes you rich in that area. Truth about God brings Spiritual riches. Truth about people brings emotional riches. Truth about yourself brings mental riches. Truth about health brings physical riches. And truth about money brings financial riches.

The proven ways that people have become millionaires are based on truths about money. The Spiritual Millionaire follows proven plans to become financially rich and learns great lessons about money. Once you learn truths about money then God can give you new ideas on how to make millions. However, God can't give you ideas on how to become a Spiritual Millionaire until you believe that you can. The proven ways of becoming a millionaire give you hope and teach you that you can. And when you believe that you can, then God can and will help you.

God can't give you ideas when you doubt. The first chapter in the book of James says, "If anyone lacks wisdom let him ask of God, who gives to all men freely and it will be given to him. But let him ask in faith, not doubting, for he who doubts is like a wave of the sea, driven and tossed by the wind. Let not that man think that he will receive anything from the Lord. He is a double-minded man unstable in all his ways. "

God will not give you ideas on how to become a Spiritual Millionaire if you doubt that you can become one. Believing that you can become a Spiritual Millionaire is one truth that you must believe before God will help you. Once you believe, then God will give you ideas so that you can see how to succeed at financial wealth.

You must also believe that you *will* become a Spiritual Millionaire. Believing you *can* do something is one level of faith, believing that you *will* do something is a higher level of faith. The Spirit of Wisdom makes Spiritual Millionaires by showing them one truth, then a brighter truth, then a brighter truth. The more you get to know the Spirit of Wisdom the more truth She will show you. The more truth you believe, the more light you will have to see how to become a Spiritual Millionaire. The more truths you learn about money the more hope you will have that you can accumulate it and the more faith you will develop that you will

28

accumulate it. The Spirit of Wisdom teaches you that you can and will become a Spiritual Millionaire when you live by faith and hope.

The Spirit of Wisdom teaches you to apply your knowledge to gain understanding. Spiritual Millionaires understand how to make money. Understanding how to do something brings faith that you will do it. Faith is empowered by understanding.

People who understand how to acquire money love to do it. Love is the next step after faith and hope. Love flows into your life when you learn to live by faith and hope. Spiritual Millionaires love God, people, themselves, and what they do to accumulate money. The Spirit of Wisdom teaches you to live with faith, hope, and love. These are the three powers of a Spiritual Millionaire's life. Faith, hope, and love will make you rich in every area of your life.

What is Faith? Faith is trust. Trust in what? Trust in God. God is love. Faith is trusting in God's love. Why does God want you to be rich? Simply, because He loves you. The Spirit of Wisdom teaches you to love by showing you that you are loved. The Spiritual Millionaires have absolute faith that God loves them. Their faith causes them to experience God's love and the experience empowers them to love themselves and others.

When you have learned to love others, the Spirit of Wisdom will show you how to become rich. When ou truly love others then you will use money for the right reasons. God trusts people who have learned how to love. Don't you trust the people who love you? Wouldn't you do whatever you could for them? Of course you would. God loves to be trusted. Spiritual Millionaires becomes successful by trusting in God to direct them. "Trust in God with all your heart, and lean not on your own understanding. In all your ways acknowledge Him and He will direct your paths. [Proverbs 3:5-6]

Remember Wisdom is the ability to make the right decisions. Faith and trusting in God is always the right decision. It is always right to love. Making the decision to live by faith and to love God, yourself, and others will lead you to becoming a Spiritual Millionaire. Faith, hope, and love make people rich. Loving God and people brings spiritual and emotional riches. Loving yourself and your body brings mental and physical riches. And loving what you do to make money, and what you can do for others with money, brings financial riches. The Spirit of Wisdom makes you rich by teaching you how to love.

Perfect love casts out fear. Spiritual Millionaires do not bow to fear because they have the power of love. When fear comes to Spiritual Millionaires they just walk through it. Fear is an illusion. It has no power in the life of a Spiritual Millionaire. The Spiritual

Millionaire shines the light of faith, hope, and love into the darkness of fear and fear disappears. Darkness cannot overpower light. Fear cannot overpower faith, hope, and love. Faith is action. Fear is inaction.

The only way fear can keep you from becoming rich is if you don't have faith, hope, and love. Spiritual Millionaires look fear in the face and choose to trust in God. Their trust in God causes them to act in spite of fear. Spiritual Millionaires use fear as a tool to make their faith, hope, and love stronger. There is no greater power than love. It is the power that a Spiritual Millionaire uses to become rich. Trying to get rich without love is a road of pain and misery. The Spirit of Wisdom teaches how to get rich by using the power of Love. Love is the source of the greatest pleasure you can know. Have faith that God loves you and wants you to be rich and the Spirit of Wisdom will show you how to become a Spiritual Millionaire.

Chapter Three

MOTIVATED BY LOVE

Happy is the man who finds Wisdom and the man who gains understanding. For her proceeds are better than the profits of silver, and her gain better than fine gold. She is more precious than rubies and all the things you may desire cannot compare with her. Long life is in her right hand; in her left hand are riches and honor. Her ways are ways of pleasantness and all her paths are peace.

[Proverbs 3:13-17]

WHAT DO YOU want and why do you want it? Answering these two questions honestly is the first step to achieving what you want in any area of your life. Knowing what you want gives you a certain level of power to move towards attaining it. Knowing why you want it gives you greater power to achieve your desires.

Motives are the empowering force to achieve your desires. If there are things you want but aren't achieving, it's because you don't have strong enough motives for achieving them. Since becoming a Spiritual Millionaire is the theme of this book let me ask these two questions related to money: How much money do you want? Why do you want it?

God is not concerned with how much money you want as much as He is concerned with why you want it. He doesn't mind if you want one million or if you want one billion. He just wants to know why you want it.

If your reasons for wanting money are pleasing to God, then the Spirit of Wisdom will help you get it. Wanting money for the right reasons will move God to act on your behalf and give you ideas on how to create wealth. Your motives are the heart of the matter.

Spiritual Millionaires have strong motives for wanting financial abundance. Strong motives empower people to become rich. There are many motives for becoming a millionaire. You might desire to become a millionaire because you want to live a comfortable life. You might desire luxury cars, big homes, and exotic vacations. There is nothing wrong with wanting nice things for yourself. The problem is in wanting them only for yourself. Spiritual Millionaires are not selfish. Being selfish is a sure way to finding misery. Being generous is a sure way to enjoy your life. Spiritual Millionaires enjoy making money and sharing it with others. Spiritual Millionaires want and use their money for the purpose of helping people know God better and improving the quality of life for humanity.

The Spiritual Millionaire is motivated by love. Love for God and all people and all things. Love is the greatest motivating force in the universe. It is not selfish. Love is the reason Spiritual Millionaires want financial abundance. They love to make money and use it to show God's love to the world.

God is Spirit. He is love. Love is spiritual and when you choose to love you have chosen to be spiritual. Becoming a Spiritual Millionaire starts with the decision to love. You were created with the desire for

36

love. The full experience of love is to be loved and to love. Selfishness is about only wanting to be loved. Success is about being loved and showing love to others.

God loves everyone, but not everyone believes it. The Spiritual Millionaire believes that God loves him. It is the belief and faith that God loves them that empowers Spiritual Millionaires to be successful in every area of their lives. You can't become a Spiritual Millionaire without absolute faith in God's love for you. God enjoys blessing people financially. The Scripture declares that God takes pleasure in the prosperity of His servant. [Psalms 35:27]

God's love is unconditional but His blessings are not. He loves you for who you are; He blesses you for what you do. There is a personal and impersonal side to spiritual life. The personal side of spiritual life is God's love. It is your purpose to experience God's love personally. The impersonal side of spiritual life is the universal laws that God has set in place. The laws of the universe work for everyone who will work them. If you follow the laws of the universe you will become successful. Take the law of sowing and reaping for instance. The law doesn't care who does the sowing. They will reap. Many people have become millionaires through application of this law. The Spiritual Millionaire not only follows the laws of the universe but also knows God personally.

Using universal truths to become wealthy without knowing God personally is not true prosperity. Success without fulfillment is failure. Universal truths can bring you success but only God can bring you fulfillment. There is a certain level of fulfillment that you get just by following the laws of the universe, but there is a much deeper level of fulfillment that comes from knowing and experiencing God personally.

You can experience success by following the laws of the universe but you will experience unconditional love by knowing God personally. The Spiritual Millionaire desires the experience of being loved by God and showing His love to others. The Spiritual Millionaire is motivated by love and desires wealth for the purposes of sharing God's love. If you are motivated by love then God will be your partner in creating wealth. Being willing to use money for the reasons that God wants you to, opens the door to the abundance of the universe.

One of the great definitions of love is that love is patient. Patience with God, people, and yourself creates rich relationships. Patience can also make you a millionaire. It takes patience to become a millionaire on compounded interest. It takes patience to wait for a piece of real estate to appreciate. It takes patience to build a business.

Patience is part of your spiritual riches. Practicing

patience can make you a Spiritual Millionaire. Even if God gives you a new idea to make millions, it will require patience for the idea to become a reality. Patience produces prosperity.

Patience is an incredibly important part of life. Many people never become rich because they are impatient. Some people, actually most people, can't wait to spend any money they get. Poverty is often the result of impulse buying. Buying things on impulse usually leads to buying things you don't really need.

If the money people spent buying things they don't need was invested over a period of time, it could make them millionaires. Investing the money you spend on soft drinks and candy bars can significantly contribute to acquiring a million dollars over a period of time. You may say, "But I enjoy the sweets and treats." Would you enjoy being a millionaire more? The Spiritual Millionaire can wait for things he wants.

Prosperity is a close friend of patience. Poverty is a close friend of impatience. Becoming a Spiritual Millionaire requires patience. Love is willing to wait when it needs to.

Two more aspects of love that can make you rich are not getting easily angered and being forgiving. The Spiritual Millionaire does not anger easily. Many people are poor today because they don't control their tempers. Anger destroys relationships, and it takes good relationships to become rich. If you want to be a Spiritual Millionaire you will need people to help you. Anger keeps people from developing the relationships that they need.

Also, forgiveness is a way of life for Spiritual Millionaires. Forgiveness allows relationships to continue and grow stronger.

You can become a Spiritual Millionaire by practicing patience, not getting easily angered, and being forgiving. Spiritual Millionaires love people the way that God loves them. People can sense love. They can also sense impatience, anger and, blame. People go out of their way to help Spiritual Millionaires because they sense love flowing through them. People avoid helping others who seem impatient and angry. If you want to be a Spiritual Millionaire then you must love unconditionally by showing patience, tolerance, and forgiveness.

Chapter Four

HUMBLE HEART AND AN OPEN MIND

Happy is the man who finds Wisdom and the man who gains understanding. For her proceeds are better than the profits of silver, and her gain better than fine gold. She is more precious than rubies and all the things you may desire cannot compare with her. Long life is in her right hand; in her left hand are riches and honor. Her ways are ways of pleasantness and all her paths are peace.

[Proverbs 3:13-17]

ASPIRITUAL MILLIONAIRE has a humble heart and an open mind. Being humble is being teachable. Part of learning is being corrected. The Spiritual Millionaire welcomes correction. Fools hate to be corrected. They don't receive correction and get angry when someone tries to help them by correcting them. Being unable to receive correction keeps people poor in every area of life.

Humility is the greatest asset a Spiritual Millionaire possesses. Through humility you can learn anything you need to know to become rich. The Spiritual Millionaire welcomes correction quickly, without getting defensive.

Arrogance is the path to poverty. Humility is the path to prosperity. Having a humble heart allows you to keep an open mind. An open mind is essential to becoming a Spiritual Millionaire. You must be willing to look at things from different points of views to become rich.

One of the reasons that some people never hear from God is because they are close-minded. When you are close-minded, you aren't teachable and willing to consider what someone else says that is different than what you believe.

It takes faith to earn money. For faith to grow you must have a humble heart and an open mind. When faith grows so does your bank account. People who make the same amount of money year after year stay at the same level of faith year after year. Correction allows people to grow and expand into higher levels of life.

Think about a child in school. He gets corrected on his work all the time and if he doesn't learn then he stays at the same level. If you are arrogant and unwilling to be corrected then you too stay on the same level of life-although eventually you will fall to a lower level. Spiritual Millionaires become abundantly wealthy because they receive correction and learn from their mistakes.

The Spirit of Wisdom brings correction to those who are willing to receive it. Scripture says, "God disciplines every child that He loves." The Spirit of Wisdom says, "Turn at my rebuke and I will pour out my Spirit on you." [Proverbs 1:23] The rebuke of Wisdom, or the discipline of God, is the way of life for a Spiritual millionaire. Spiritual Millionaires actually look for correction.

King Solomon wrote most of the book of Proverbs. He was blessed with the Spirit of Wisdom because he asked for it. Part of asking God for His Spirit of

Wisdom is to ask for correction. Solomon's father, King David, learned of the benefits of receiving correction. In Psalms he said to God, "Your righteous judgments are to be more desired than fine gold." Looking for and receiving correction will lead you to become a Spiritual Millionaire.

Receiving correction is to admit that you were wrong or that what you're thinking and doing is not the best way to think or act. Spiritual Millionaires admit they are wrong when they realize they are. They are able to know when they are wrong because they have open minds. Being close-minded keeps you from being able to see better ways to think and act. Close-minded people miss the benefits of learning because they refuse to look at things from a different point of view. Many people live in poverty their entire lives because they are arrogant and narrow-minded. You can become rich by being humble and keeping your mind open to all possibilities. Having an open mind allows you to receive information from the Spirit of Wisdom on how to create wealth.

Spiritual Millionaires look for possibilities not problems. There are an infinite number of possibilities that God could give you on how to become financially wealthy. With God all things are possible. Nothing is impossible to those who believe. Spiritual Millionaires believe that God can and will give them ideas and opportunities on how to get rich. Because they believe it, they receive it. When the Spirit of Wisdom gives you an idea, it often means you have to do things differently than you did them before. Not all correction means you did something wrong. Most of the instruction Spiritual millionaires receive is on how to do things better. Being humble and open-minded allows you to accept this correction.

The problem that many people experience is not having enough ideas. Spiritual Millionaires have a problem too, but it's a good problem. They have too many ideas. New ideas flow like a river through the minds of Spiritual Millionaires. They always have something they can do to make money.

Spiritual Millionaires have to be careful about trying to do too much. They should keep focused on a just few things and let others do the rest. This is an area that many Spiritual Millionaires receive correction in often.

Remember, being able to accept correction is an important part of becoming a Spiritual Millionaire. Listening to correction from anyone at anytime allows the Spirit of Wisdom to correct you quickly before a situation can worsen. The Spirit of Wisdom can save you from mistakes when you listen.

Being humble is a learned behavior; it is not natural for humans to be humble. The Spirit of Wisdom must teach you humility before She can teach you how to become a millionaire. Millionaires who are not humble have acquired their wealth through the universal principles concerning money but they do not have the deep inner peace that the Spiritual Millionaire has. The deep inner peace of God comes through applying the universal principles in every area of life. When you try to use the universal principles of God in the area of money, before the more important areas of life, then the Spirit of Wisdom brings correction.

God wants you to do the right things at the right time with the right people. Being humble and open-minded allows you to see the order in which you should do things. There is a divine order to becoming a Spiritual Millionaire. Our idea of order is often different than God's idea of order. Our logical minds think if we had more money then we would do more good. God's order, however, is the opposite. If you do good, then you will have more money. Doing good in your spiritual, emotional, mental, and physical life will lead you to doing extremely well in your financial life. Listen for the Spirit of Wisdom to bring correction into the more important areas of your life. If you will heed Her correction She will lead you to becoming a Spiritual Millionaire that has deep inner peace and joy, as well as abundant finances.

Chapter Five

LETTING IT GO

Happy is the man who finds Wisdom and the man who gains understanding. For her proceeds are better than the profits of silver, and her gain better than fine gold. She is more precious than rubies and all the things you may desire cannot compare with her. Long life is in her right hand; in her left hand are riches and honor. Her ways are ways of pleasantness and all her paths are peace.

[Proverbs 3:13-17]

SPIRITUAL MILLIONAIRES LIKE accumulating money and they enjoy the things that money can buy—but they aren't attached to any of it. They can let it all go. Their relationship with God means more to them than their material possessions. They are more concerned with the presence of God in their lives than the balance in their bank accounts and the things they own.

You must be willing to let go of your money and possessions if you want to become a Spiritual Millionaire. There are times when God will require Spiritual Millionaires to give things away, including large amounts of money. This is an easy task for Spiritual Millionaires because on their way to becoming wealthy they learned how to give.

A Spiritual millionaire is generous. They became this way from listening to the Spirit of Wisdom when they only had small amounts of money. The Spirit of Wisdom teaches you to be faithful with little so you can one day be trusted with much. People who do not faithfully give, even when they aren't making much money, can never become a Spiritual Millionaire.

Spiritual Millionaires know they are just a steward of the things they possess. Not only do they not mind letting go of things and money when God tells them to, they actually enjoy it. They understand that God is their source and He will always provide for them. They know God will show them how to create more wealth if they give. The joy of accumulating money and the joy of giving it away is a continuous circle in the life of a Spiritual Millionaire.

When you become a Spiritual Millionaire you will be required to let go of more than just money. You will be required to let go of jobs, businesses, investments, and other sources of income.

There are two main reasons for this. One is because when you have a certain business or job for a while you may start to think that the business or job is your source. And two, many of the jobs and businesses you are involved in are just training grounds for bigger and better things.

Many Spiritual Millionaires have had to let go of their jobs and businesses so that God could move them on to other opportunities. The Spiritual Millionaire lets go of something good for something better.

Most jobs and businesses have a cap on how much money you can earn from them. To move into the world of true financial abundance you will have to leave behind the jobs and businesses that limit your income. The Spiritual Millionaire is always looking for ways to increase his income.

The Spirit of Wisdom tells you when it is time to move on. When you have learned what you needed to from certain jobs or businesses or when you have reached the place where your income is being limited, it is time to change. Spiritual Millionaires can leave a job or business because they know there is a better one coming.

Sometimes knowing the Spirit of Wisdom will allow you to see the better opportunity before you have to leave your current job or business, but not always. People who have been laid off or failed at a business venture often don't see what's next because they aren't looking for it. Since Spiritual Millionaires are always looking for ways to make more money they usually see the better opportunity before they have to let go of their current job or business. Being laid off or failing at a business attempt is often just God reminding you that He is your source or He is trying to get you to the next level. The Spirit of Wisdom teaches you how to hold all things loosely because there may be a time when you have to let them go.

The Spiritual Millionaire is able to let go of things because they live by faith. They know, without a doubt, that God will provide. Fear makes people hold onto things that prevent them from growing. Faith will move you forward. Fear holds you back. Faith lets go and fear holds on.

If you want to be a Spiritual Millionaire you will have to let go of certain things. Keep in mind that your current job or business may just be a season of your life. Continue to look for better ways that you enjoy to earn more money.

One of the signs that a season is about to end is when you become discontent. A little discontent usually doesn't mean that it's time to move on. A little discontent is usually just a sign from God trying to teach you to be content. Spiritual Millionaires have mastered the art of being content with what they have, while being in pursuit of what they want. They are content with where they are but always looking for where God will take them next.

When you have learned to appreciate what you have and where you are, then the time is close for you to let go and move on to the next level. There is always a higher level. But you can't go to the next level until you leave the one you're on. This is where the Spirit of Wisdom will give you divine discontentment.

Divine discontent is deeper and stronger than just being uncomfortable or somewhat displeased with your current situation. It is being deeply discontent and not understanding why you feel this way because everything seems to be going so well. It is when you know you should be content but for some unknown reason you just aren't. It is a strange feeling of not knowing why you feel the way you do.

Divine discontent comes because you are ready to learn deeper truths about God, yourself, and money. Without this divine discontent you would become satisfied with less than God's best for you.

Spiritual Millionaires enjoy the best that life has to offer. Be willing to let go of what you have and where you are, and the Spirit of Wisdom will show you the right time to do it.

Most Spiritual Millionaires have had to let go of many jobs and businesses to increase their income. The lessons they learned from past jobs and businesses prepared them for more financial prosperity. What are the lessons God is trying to teach you in your present circumstances? Learn them well, and the Spirit of Wisdom will tell you when to let go, so you can rise to the next level. There is always more that God wants to show you. Letting go of what lies behind allows you to see what's ahead. Turn your back on yesterday and face the future with the Spirit of Wisdom.

We don't have eyes in the back of our heads because God doesn't want us looking behind us. Look forward to better things and they will start to come. The Spirit of Wisdom will show you the way if you stop looking at what has already happened. A Spiritual

Millionaire let's go of what lies behind and reaches for what lies ahead.

Chapter Six

DEEP DESIRES

Happy is the man who finds Wisdom and the man who gains understanding. For her proceeds are better than the profits of silver, and her gain better than fine gold. She is more precious than rubies and all the things you may desire cannot compare with her. Long life is in her right hand; in her left hand are riches and honor. Her ways are ways of pleasantness and all her paths are peace.

[Proverbs 3:13-17]

HAVE YOU EVER wanted something terribly and then, once you acquired it, realized you didn't want it that much after all? The majority of people in the world spend most of their time, energy, and money seeking to fulfill deceptive desires. Spiritual Millionaires seek to find, follow, and fulfill the deep desires that God has put into their hearts.

A deceptive desire is something that you think will bring you fulfillment, but when you achieve it, it doesn't. Your deepest desires are the purposes for which you were created. Fulfilling your purposes produces the greatest fulfillment in life. The Spirit of Wisdom makes people rich by helping them fulfill their purposes.

The deep desires of your life are often suppressed by deceptive desires. Or stated another way, the purposes of your life are often suppressed by things that are not your purposes. This happens because we live in a world where our senses are constantly bombarded with advertisements of products that promise to make us feel successful and happy. A

Spiritual Millionaire is aware of this deception and is careful what he or she allows to go into his or her mind. It is inevitable that some deceptive desires will enter our minds, but we can learn to discern between the deep desires of our heart and the deceptive desires of our mind.

Spiritual Millionaires seek to live life from their hearts. They are aware that seeing the same product advertised again and again can influence them. The way the Spiritual Millionaire combats this is by bombarding his mind with the desires of his heart.

Whichever desires you feed, you will fulfill. You feed a desire by thinking about it. The more you think about a desire, the more likely you are to fulfill it. It is important to keep the deepest desires of your heart in your mind as much as you possibly can. The mind goes to work on whatever you give it. If you allow the world to give it desires for things that you don't really want or need, then you will find yourself spending your time, energy, and money going after them. If you allow the Spirit of Wisdom to fill your mind with the purposes for which you were created, then you will fulfill your purposes and find peace and prosperity.

Your deep desires give you purpose and a passion for living. They are what drive the Spiritual Millionaire to become rich in every area of life. Desiring to be rich in every area of life is deep.

Desiring money alone is shallow. Being deep or shallow is a choice. The Spirit of Wisdom gives you the power to make the right choice and desire the right things. Desire is a choice. If you want something today it is because you made a choice to want it at some point. The Spirit of Wisdom encourages you to desire the deep things while the world wants you to desire shallow things. Choose to follow the deep desires of your heart.

God puts deep desires in your heart and the world puts deceptive desires in your mind. Choose the deep desires and the Spirit of Wisdom will show you how to fulfill them. Choose the deceptive desires and the foolishness of the world will keep you from achieving any true success. The deep desires of your heart are to be rich in every area of your life. To fulfill the deep desires of your heart you have to keep them in your mind. Your mind can only hold one thought at a time. You can't desire the deep things and the deceptive things at the same time. If you keep the deep desires of your heart in your mind consistently, then you will not waste your time, energy, and money pursuing things that won't fulfill you.

A Spiritual Millionaire is successful because he keeps his deep desires in his mind consistently. He has chosen to be rich in every area of his life. If you want to be a Spiritual Millionaire you must choose to follow the deep desires of your heart. Spiritual Millionaires do not get sidetracked by the deceptive desires that run through their minds. The Spirit of Wisdom has taught them to train their minds to think about being rich in every area of life.

If you keep the deep desires of your heart in your mind then the deceptive desires of this world will not be able to distract you from you becoming a Spiritual Millionaire. You must train your mind to consistently think about your deepest desires so that you become rich in every area of your life.

Chapter Seven

TRAINING YOUR MIND

Happy is the man who finds Wisdom and the man who gains understanding. For her proceeds are better than the profits of silver, and her gain better than fine gold. She is more precious than rubies and all the things you may desire cannot compare with her. Long life is in her right hand; in her left hand are riches and honor. Her ways are ways of pleasantness and all her paths are peace.

[Proverbs 3:13-17]

THE SPIRITUAL MILLIONAIRE disciplines his mind to think about those things that will make him rich in every area of life. Disciplining one's mind is a lifelong process. Spiritual Millionaires are committed to lifelong learning. They keep a constant flow of positive ideas and thoughts going into their minds. One way they do this is by reading books and listening to audio programs by people who have achieved the results that they want in their lives.

The Spirit of Wisdom leads Spiritual Millionaires to people who can teach them what they want and need to know. By reading and listening to others you can compress time and learn something in a few hours that took someone else years to learn. A Spiritual Millionaire has many teachers who help him train his mind.

Athletes train their bodies to do what they want them to do by doing the same thing over and over again. To train your mind you must think about the same things over and over.

The way your mind has been trained to think determines the results you get in your life. If you don't train your mind, someone else will do it for you. The Spiritual Millionaire is always training her mind to serve her better.

Training requires repetition. You must constantly bombard your mind with thoughts of success. You must keep your mind saturated with positive thoughts. When you find a book or audio program that speaks to your heart, listen to it over and over again. Repetition is a powerful way to train your mind. When you hear something that you have already heard, NEVER say, "I already know that." You need to be reminded of certain truths again and again. If someone recommends a book to you that you have already read, it may be the Spirit of Wisdom telling you that you need to read it again. The Spirit of Wisdom constantly reminds the Spiritual Millionaire to keep thinking thoughts of purpose, peace, and prosperity. The Spiritual Millionaire becomes rich by conditioning her mind to attract riches. She keeps prospering because she keeps thinking prosperous thoughts.

Have you ever noticed that the same situations keep repeating themselves in your life? The reason this happens is because your mind has been conditioned to think in a certain way. Once something has been repeated numerous times, your mind will continue to think in the same way and produce the same results. This is true of positive and negative thoughts.

Many of the negative things people keep going through again and again is the result of their minds thinking the same negative thoughts over and over. Once you have trained your mind to think in a certain way it will keep repeating the same thoughts and you will keep getting the same results in your life, negative or positive.

The Spirit of Wisdom teaches you to think the right thoughts, which produce the right actions, which produce the right results. If you do not listen to the Spirit of Wisdom then the world will train your mind to think wrong thoughts, that will produce wrong actions and wrong results.

If your mind has been trained to think thoughts that produce bad results, then you will have to retrain your mind. Sometimes you must unlearn what you have learned. If an athlete practices a movement or skill the wrong way, he will learn to do the movement or skill improperly. The saying "practice makes perfect" is only true if it is proper practice. Your mind can harbor thoughts that you think are positive but if they are not producing the results you want, then you must retrain your mind to think differently.

You won't get different results in your life until you change the thinking that was causing the results you were getting. Positive thoughts produce positive results. Negative thoughts produce negative results.

Positive thoughts lead you to peace and fulfillment; negative thoughts lead you to stress and depression.

If you are getting results in your life that you don't want, it is because you have not trained your mind to think about what you do want. This may sound too simple to be true, but it is. Your mind has the power to make you rich or poor. Rich thoughts make you rich. Poor thoughts make you poor. The Spiritual Millionaire is constantly training and retraining his mind to think thoughts that will make him richer and richer.

The differences between the poor, the middle class, the rich, and the super rich are just differences in the way they think. To become a Spiritual Millionaire you must let the Spirit of Wisdom teach you how to think. Be open to Her correction. When you are thinking things that you shouldn't, the result will be stress, confusion, worry, or fear. The thoughts that will make you a Spiritual Millionaire produce peace, understanding, and faith.

Any time you experience a negative emotion consider it a rebuke from the Spirit of Wisdom and realize that you are thinking negative thoughts. Pay close attention to the thoughts you have. Training your mind to serve you on your quest to become a Spiritual Millionaire will require you to be aware of your thoughts. It will also require you to quickly find and replace the thoughts that produce negative results in your life. Positive thoughts give you inner light for inner sight. Negative thoughts turn out the lights on your purposes.

Training your mind will allow you to see clearly what to do next in your life and how to do it. The Spirit of Wisdom gives you vision for your life by training your mind to think about your purposes.

Spiritual Millionaires become rich by thinking about their purposes constantly. Likewise, you will act on the thoughts that you have consistently. Become aware of your thoughts and pay close attention to what you are thinking. Your mind can be your greatest friend or your worst enemy. Train your mind to become the person you were created to be. The day you decide to train your mind and be conscious of the thoughts you are thinking is the day that becoming a Spiritual Millionaire becomes possible. Spiritual Millionaires never stop training their minds.

A well-trained mind is a strong mind. It overcomes thoughts of fear, doubt, and worry. An untrained mind falls prey to the fears, lies, and unbelief of others. When you have trained your mind you will have learned how to think for yourself. Being able to think for yourself empowers you to make your own decisions.

Don't let other people decide who you should be, what you should do, or what you should have in life.

Letting other people think for you and decide what you should be, do, and have will give you a *shouldy* life. Your personal purposes can only be fulfilled by you.

Train your mind to think about the desires of your heart. Having a well-trained mind allows you to make decisions that are in line with your personal purposes quickly and easily. Spiritual Millionaires seek wise counsel from others but they don't let others tell them what they can or can't do. A person with an untrained mind is always looking to someone else to make things happen for him. A trained mind will make things happen for you.

It takes faith to become rich in every area of life. It takes faith to make money. A well-trained mind has faith. An untrained mind has fear. The Spiritual Millionaire's mind is full of faith. Faith is the greatest benefit of a trained mind. When you continually think positive thoughts then faith, hope, and love empower you to become a Spiritual Millionaire.

What is a positive thought? A positive thought is a truth. The Spirit of Wisdom teaches you to think about truth. Lies produce fear, doubt, and worry. Lies are spiritual darkness that keep you from seeing how to become a Spiritual Millionaire. Truth is spiritual light that allows you to see. Train your mind with truth.

When you experience fear, doubt, stress, and worry you are thinking about lies. Light overcomes darkness.

Spiritual Millionaires overcome lies with truth; they overcome fear with faith. Training your mind with truth gives you the faith to accomplish the desires of your heart.

There are absolute truths that exist for everyone and there are also personal truths that deal with your personal purposes. A Spiritual Millionaire follows universal and personal truths. Train your mind with universal and personal truths and you will become a Spiritual Millionaire.

You can learn many of the universal truths from successful people but only the Spirit of Wisdom can teach you the personal truths for your life. Training your mind is your personal responsibility. If you want to become a Spiritual Millionaire you must continually train your mind to think about your personal purposes in life. Listen to the Spirit of Wisdom and She will teach you how to train your mind and make you rich.

Chapter Eight

PRAYER AND MEDITATION

Happy is the man who finds Wisdom and the man who gains understanding. For her proceeds are better than the profits of silver, and her gain better than fine gold. She is more precious than rubies and all the things you may desire cannot compare with her. Long life is in her right hand; in her left hand are riches and honor. Her ways are ways of pleasantness and all her paths are peace.

[Proverbs 3:13-17]

PRAYER AND MEDITATION form the foundation of the Spiritual Millionaire's life. There are many definitions of what prayer is and what meditation is. Explaining prayer and meditation can be somewhat involved, but I will use simple definitions for them here. Prayer is talking to God and meditation is listening to God. Prayer is talking about your desires with God and meditation is God talking about His desires with you.

If you take the time to talk with God and listen for Him to talk with you, then you will have the power to become a Spiritual Millionaire. Many people never hear from the Spirit of Wisdom simply because they don't listen for Her to speak to them.

Prayer without meditation is not effective in discovering your purposes for life. Prayer without meditation is like trying to fly a kite without wind. You absolutely must take the time to meditate to become successful. The Spiritual Millionaire understands that prayer and meditation are keys to their success.

Spiritual Millionaires pray and meditate all the time. They don't look at these two things as religious activities but rather as a lifestyle choice. Prayer and meditation are the start and finish of the Spiritual Millionaire's day and they are also a part of everything in between.

The Spiritual Millionaire looks at prayer and meditation as an attitude and a way of life, not just something he does. It is not just a part of what he does, it is a part of who he is. By living every moment of life as a prayer and always listening for God to speak to him, he lives in the Spiritual state that we call faith.

To live by faith is to walk with the Spirit of Wisdom every moment. Prayer and meditation keep you on the path of purpose, peace, and prosperity. Meditation is the place where God reveals to you the purposes for your life and how to accomplish them.

Meditation shows respect to the Spirit of Wisdom. How would you feel if someone only wanted to talk with you but didn't want to listen to you? Is that not disrespectful? Yet, that is how many people communicate with God. They pray and pray and pray but never take the time to listen.

The example that God gave us two ears and one mouth so that we should listen twice as much as we talk, applies to our relationships with people and to our relationship with the Spirit of Wisdom. It is amazing how much we can learn when we become good listeners. It is wonderful how much God communicates with us when we take the time to listen. Listening is one of the greatest strengths of a Spiritual Millionaire. It opens his eyes to new ideas and possibilities.

God communicates in numerous ways. He can speak to you with a quiet voice, He can give you feelings or hunches, He can speak to you through other people or a song or a movie, etc. One of the most powerful ways that God speaks is through visions. Meditation is where you receive visions. Vision is spiritual, sight is physical. Vision is internal, sight is external. Visions are mental pictures of who God wants you to become and what He wants you to do. The Spiritual Millionaire is led by visions. Visions give you an understanding of God's purposes for your life.

The more you meditate the clearer your visions become. The clearer your visions, the more likely you are to achieve them. Meditation gives you the power to bring the invisible world of your thoughts into the visible world of form. Meditation not only gives you visions but also the knowledge of how to bring the visions to pass. The Spiritual Millionaire understands what God wants him to do with his life and how to do it. Understanding what you are to do and how you are to do it gives you incredible peace of mind.

There are many benefits to making prayer and meditation a part of your lifestyle. Peace of mind is one of the greatest. Prayer and meditation also increase your faith. They are faith in action. They are proof that you believe and trust in your Creator.

It is impossible to become a Spiritual Millionaire without making prayer and meditation part of your everyday life. Scripture says without faith it is impossible to please God. Prayer and meditation is how you exercise your faith. Exercising your faith makes it grow and become stronger. The stronger your faith the richer you can become.

Plus, the infinite knowledge of God is available through prayer and meditation. The Spiritual Millionaire taps into the wisdom, knowledge, and understanding of the Creator of the universe through prayer and meditation. Prayer and meditation are not powerless religious activities. They are powerful spiritual practices. They are absolutely necessary to become a Spiritual Millionaire.

Take the time to talk with God and to listen for Him to talk with you. If you truly listen and keep an open mind you will start to become aware of the ways that God is trying to talk with you. It is not hard to hear God. All you have to do is take the time to listen.

There are many voices that speak to us. Some of the voices in your head say things to encourage you and increase your faith, hope, and love while others say things to discourage you and make you afraid, stressed, and worried. The Spiritual Millionaire has learned to listen to the voices that encourage and ignore the voices that discourage. The voices that encourage you are God, yourself, and others who love you. The voices that discourage you are from people or beings that hate you.

You can call the discouraging voices whatever you want. I believe in angels and demons. The voices that speak words of discouragement are demonic. Based on my experience, when prayer and meditation become a regular part of your life, you will start to become aware of who is speaking to you. The Spiritual Millionaire can quickly distinguish between the voice of God and the demonic voices.

When prayer and meditation are not a part of your daily life, you can mistake discouraging thoughts for your own. You are not the source of all your thoughts. When you develop sensitivity to the voice of God, you also become more sensitive to demonic voices. The voice of God produces faith. Demonic voices produce fear. The voice of God inspires, excites, and energizes you to fulfill your purposes. The Spiritual Millionaire loves prayer and meditation. It is the way he stays connected to his Source and receives what he needs to succeed.

Chapter Nine

VISUALIZING
YOUR VISION

Happy is the man who finds Wisdom and the man who gains understanding. For her proceeds are better than the profits of silver, and her gain better than fine gold. She is more precious than rubies and all the things you may desire cannot compare with her. Long life is in her right hand; in her left hand are riches and honor. Her ways are ways of pleasantness and all her paths are peace.

[Proverbs 3:13-17]

VISUALIZING GOES BEYOND meditation. When you meditate, you receive visions; when you visualize you *focus* on those visions. The visions you have while meditating show you what you need to do, and when you visualize, you see it as already done. Visualizing is using your imagination to see things as you want them to be. It is feeling them as being accomplished. When you are good at visualizing and do it often you will feel absolute certainty that your vision will come to pass because you have already seen it and felt it many times. A Spiritual Millionaire constantly visualizes his visions.

Although you can visualize during meditation, the main focus of meditating should be listening and paying attention to the pictures that go through your mind. It's best if you consider visualizing and meditating as being separate activities. If you do this, then the time spent at both activities will be more productive. During meditation open yourself to receiving new visions and obtaining better clarity of the visions you've already seen. When you visualize, just focus intensely on one particular vision.

Just as prayer and meditation are lifestyle choices for Spiritual Millionaires, so is visualizing. Visualizing, prayer, and meditation compliment each other. Let's say you receive a vision of what to do while meditating but you don't yet understand how to do it. Visualizing your vision, seeing and feeling it as done, will improve your times of meditating. The what and how of a vision come through meditation. Visualizing is beyond the what and how. It is the *now*. Seeing and feeling your vision as being completed, right now, has great influence on making the what and how come to pass quicker than you might have thought possible.

Visualizing is key to manifesting your deep desires. It opens doors to the impossible and lets miracles come into your life. The more you visualize the more you realize. Visualizing is both visual and emotional. Just seeing your vision as already done is powerful. But stirring up your emotions and developing a strong feeling that your vision has already come to pass is even more powerful.

Faith and love are the major components of visualizing. Through faith you *see* a vision as done and through love you *feel* it as done. This is why knowing and following the deep desires of your heart are so important. The deep desires that God has put inside of you are the things you have faith for and they are the things you love to do. Visualizing is an extremely enjoyable experience. It is a healthy habit in the life of a Spiritual Millionaire.

When you first start to visualize your visions you may not be able to feel them as being done. That's okay. Keep visualizing your visions on the level of just seeing them done. After a while, feelings will start to emerge. When the feelings are a part of your visualizing, start looking for the how to be revealed to you. When you have developed a consistently strong feeling of a vision as already fulfilled you are getting close to seeing it come to pass.

Your thoughts control your feelings. The more you think certain thoughts the stronger the feelings that are attached to them will become. Repetition trains your mind and your emotions. Spiritual Millionaires use their minds and emotions while visualizing.

Visualizing is one of the greatest ways to bring you closer to a completed vision in a shorter amount of time. Prayer and meditation alone can give you the power to fulfill your heart's desires, but visualizing them will definitely speed up the process.

If you want to become rich in every area of your life, then see and feel yourself as being rich right now-in all of those areas. Develop a habit of visualizing what you want many times each day. Use your mind to bring what you know will happen in the future into the present moment by visualizing. Feeling a future vision as already completed inspires and excites you. It moves you to action. Every time you get done visualizing see if there is something you can do to bring you closer to accomplishing your vision. One of the great benefits of visualizing is the energy it gives you to act on your desires. Add visualizing to your prayers and meditations and you will become a Spiritual Millionaire.

Chapter Ten

AFFIRMATIONS

Happy is the man who finds Wisdom and the man who gains understanding. For her proceeds are better than the profits of silver, and her gain better than fine gold. She is more precious than rubies and all the things you may desire cannot compare with her. Long life is in her right hand; in her left hand are riches and honor. Her ways are ways of pleasantness and all her paths are peace.

[Proverbs 3:13-17]

THE SPIRITUAL MILLIONAIRE uses affirmations to become rich. The power of affirmations is that you begin to believe what you say. When you have used certain affirmations long enough you not only develop the belief but also the feeling that what you are saying is true.

People use affirmations all the time, but are not usually aware of it. Most affirmations are used to manifest negative things. Affirmations like: I am fat. I am ugly. I am angry. I am not smart enough. I am worried. I am tired. Spiritual Millionaires are careful what they allow to come out of their mouths. If you want to become a Spiritual Millionaire you must believe that your words will eventually become your reality.

You must learn to use affirmations to become who you want to be. Whatever you attach to the words "I am" you will become. Pay close attention to the way you talk about yourself for the next week. Become aware of any negative statements that you make about yourself or your circumstances. Create affirmations that are the opposite of the negative ones you have been saying. The affirmations about who you want to become must start with "I am". Some examples are: I am loving. I am forgiving. I am patient. I am peaceful. I am healthy. I am strong.

Make your own affirmations and repeat them to yourself out loud with emotion. If you say affirmations without putting any feeling behind what you are saying, it won't work. You must energize your affirmations with emotion. When you use affirmations *believe* and *feel* them to be true.

Affirmations must be stated in the present. They do not work if you say, "*Someday* I will be rich or *someday* I will be healthy." The moment that matters is *now*. You must state your affirmations as if they are true today. In the Scriptures God calls those things that are not as though they were. Be careful not to turn that around and try to call the things that are as though they are not. That doesn't work.

Affirmations must be stated in the positive. It won't work to say, "I am not broke," if you are. What does work is to say, "I am rich. I am debt free. I am a Spiritual Millionaire!"

It is best for you to come up with your own affirmations. However, if you haven't used affirmations before, I will give you a simple one to get you started. As you become more familiar with affirmations, then develop your own with words that are most meaningful to you. For now, try saying this every day, hundreds of times, out loud, with emotion: "I am a Spiritual Millionaire. I am rich in every area of my life."

There are many ways to state affirmations. The "I am" affirmations seem to be the most powerful, but you also need to create affirmations that state the things you want to do and the things you want to have, as if you are already doing them and already have them. Some examples are: I make $1,000,000 a year. I exercise every day. I weigh ___ pounds. I have a great relationship with my spouse. I have a beautiful home in a great neighborhood.

Whatever you want to be, do, and have, create your own affirmations and use them daily. Just have fun with them and remember to believe and feel your affirmations as being true.

One of the best times to say your affirmations is while exercising. The best way to start your day is with prayer, meditation, visualizing, exercise, and saying affirmations. It is easier to develop intense feelings while exercising. Motion is linked to emotion. Have you ever noticed how emotional people can be when they are playing sports? Use motion to create emotion while you are saying your affirmations.

This may sound weird, but it works. Don't let disbelief take you out of the game before you even get to bat. Affirmations are a home run. You don't have to understand how it all works to receive the benefits. Just do it! You will be glad you did.

Chapter Eleven

PURPOSE-BASED GOALS

Happy is the man who finds Wisdom and the man who gains understanding. For her proceeds are better than the profits of silver, and her gain better than fine gold. She is more precious than rubies and all the things you may desire cannot compare with her. Long life is in her right hand; in her left hand are riches and honor. Her ways are ways of pleasantness and all her paths are peace.

[Proverbs 3:13-17]

IT IS AMAZING how many people don't have goals or don't know what they want in life. Not having goals is a sign that someone doesn't know their purpose for living. Having goals gives your life direction and meaning.

Goals based on your purpose for living have the power of God inside of them. The Spirit of Wisdom always helps you fulfill the goals for which you were created.

The Spiritual Millionaire has an abundance of goals. Goals energize, excite, and empower you to become the person you were created to be. You should have many goals.

You probably have one main lifelong purpose, and you should also have other purposes. You can have spiritual purposes based on your relationship with God. You can have emotional purposes based on your relationship with the important people in your life. You can have mental purposes that deal with your relationship with yourself and the things you should be learning about. You can have physical purposes regarding your health and how you treat your body. You can have financial purposes about how much money you can earn and how much to give away.

The Spirit of Wisdom will help you find and fulfill all of your life purposes. Spiritual Millionaires use goals to keep focused on the purposes of their lives.

You must set goals in every area of your life. What is your spiritual purpose? Set goals for developing your relationship with God and becoming more spiritual.

What are your emotional purposes? Whom are you supposed to have a relationship with? Set goals to meet and get to know those people. What kinds of relationships do you want to have with your family and friends? Set goals to develop those relationships.

What do you feel are your mental purposes? What do you think God wants you to learn about? How is your relationship with yourself? Do you have peace of mind? Set goals for your mental health. Learn about things that excite you. Make having peace of mind a goal. God wants you to have peace of mind.

What are your physical purposes? What is the ideal weight for your body? How healthy would you like to be? Set goals to be as healthy as you can be.

What are your financial purposes? How much money would you like to make? How much money would you like to donate to causes you believe in? What are you supposed to be doing to make money? Set goals to create financial abundance. Set a goal to become a Spiritual Millionaire. Set a goal for how much money you want to donate each year. Set a goal for the kind of job or business you want.

Remember your purposes can be discovered in the deep desires of your heart. The desires that inspire you are often what God is calling you to do. The Spirit of Wisdom will help you acquire everything you want. Just decide what you do want, set goals based on your purposes, and focus on them daily. Have the courage to follow God and the desires He has put in your heart.

Goals must be prayed about, meditated on, visualized, and affirmed on a daily basis. Write your goals down. This is important. I suggest keeping a journal of your goals and adding to them continually. Pray over them. Listen to God for plans on how to achieve them. Visualize them coming to pass. Use positive affirmations stated in the present tense. Feel yourself becoming, doing, and having all that God wants for you. Never settle for less than the purposes for which you were created.

You can and will have the life you desire when you set goals based on your purposes. When setting your goals, dream big. Be flexible and change your goals as you need to. Write your goals down once a week. Read them out loud every day. Create fun affirmations based on your goals and repeat them out loud over and over again.

Having a "goal board" can help you visualize your goals. A goal board is where you hang pictures of the places you want to visit; the people you want to meet; the activities you want to do; the charities you want to support; and the things you want to purchase, like cars, motorcycles, houses, furniture, etc. Find pictures of anything and everything related to your goals. Display them where you will look at them every day. Imagine how it feels to be, do, and have what you see in the pictures.

Prayer, meditation, visualizing, affirming, writing down goals, and creating a goal board will help you fulfill your purposes faster than you ever dreamed possible. You don't have to settle for less. Start living the life you were created for. Set goals based on your purposes and the Spirit of Wisdom will show you how to make them happen.

Chapter Twelve

SUCCESSFUL FAILURES

Happy is the man who finds Wisdom and the man who gains understanding. For her proceeds are better than the profits of silver, and her gain better than fine gold. She is more precious than rubies and all the things you may desire cannot compare with her. Long life is in her right hand; in her left hand are riches and honor. Her ways are ways of pleasantness and all her paths are peace.

[Proverbs 3:13-17]

THE SPIRITUAL MILLIONAIRE knows that failure is often a part of success. He knows that failure is temporary. It is not eternal. Failure to Spiritual Millionaires isn't failure in the traditional sense of the word. To them it is a learning experience. Failure is only failure if you don't learn something from it. If you learn a lesson that helps you succeed on something else, then whatever you seemingly failed at was actually a success! A successful failure is something that didn't go quite according to plan—but in the process the Spirit of Wisdom was able to teach you something that you needed to know.

Spiritual Millionaires see failure as their teacher. They don't mind when they fail because they will always learn from the blunder and are better for it. Something is not a failure if you learn from it. The Spiritual Millionaire doesn't take failure personally. He knows that failure is something he did, not something he is.

People who feel like they are failures will never become Spiritual Millionaires. You must be able to separate yourself from the failure and not identify it as being a part of who you are—instead look upon it as something you tried that didn't work.

If you see *failure* as a verb and not a noun you will be able to learn from it and become better, stronger, and wiser. Every Spiritual Millionaire has failed many times. It is the failures that help make Spiritual Millionaires as successful as they are. Without failure Spiritual Millionaires would not have learned things that were absolutely necessary for the successes that they enjoy today.

If you learn from a failure then it is actually a success. Whether or not you become more successful from the failure depends on if you use what you learned to try again. The lessons you learn from failures only make you better if you apply what you learned.

A Spiritual Millionaire never quits, that's why she becomes rich. If you quit after a failure then you didn't learn the lesson. A lesson is only learned through application. The first part of a lesson from a failure is the knowledge that you get. The second part of the lesson, which is the part that makes you rich, is applying what you learned and trying again.

Wisdom is the application of knowledge. The knowledge you gain from a failure must be applied if you want to become a Spiritual Millionaire.

Some Spiritual Millionaires have failed on the same project over and over again. The Spiritual Millionaire, however, is willing to try again and again, on the same idea. They just make small changes along the way. Think of Thomas Edison trying to invent the light bulb. He failed 10,000 times but always kept trying. Most people quit after just one failure. Persistence always pays off if you learn along the way.

Through failure you discover what doesn't work. Being willing to fail more than once will eventually help you find what does work—as long as you keep trying. What you shouldn't do is keep doing the same thing over and over again. You must change something before you do it again. The change has to be based on the lesson you learned on a prior failure. If you are willing to learn from your failures and try again you will eventually succeed. Spiritual Millionaires become rich by learning valuable lessons from their failures and using the knowledge they gain to try again.

You must be willing to fail and try again to become a Spiritual Millionaire.

Timing is critical to success. Many ideas become failures simply because they were acted on at the wrong time. Sometimes it is not *what* you did that failed but *when* you did it. The Spiritual Millionaire is aware of this and tries to do the right things at the right times.

Whether you apply timing to buying real estate or stocks or starting a new business, knowing when to act will make you rich. You need to know when to buy and when to sell. This is perhaps one of the greatest benefits of knowing the Spirit of Wisdom. She always knows the right times to act. She knows when you should wait and when you should move. Listen to the Spirit of Wisdom concerning the right times to do things and She will make you rich.

Chapter Thirteen

WHO ARE YOU BECOMING?

Happy is the man who finds Wisdom and the man who gains understanding. For her proceeds are better than the profits of silver, and her gain better than fine gold. She is more precious than rubies and all the things you may desire cannot compare with her. Long life is in her right hand; in her left hand are riches and honor. Her ways are ways of pleasantness and all her paths are peace.

[Proverbs 3:13-17]

THE GREATEST BENEFIT of becoming a Spiritual Millionaire is not the money but who you become in the process. You become a person of love. The more loving you become, the richer you become. In order to become a Spiritual Millionaire you must develop a strong faith in God. The stronger your faith, the richer you become.

During the process of becoming a Spiritual Millionaire you will develop many wonderful relationships with people who are on the same path as you. The more relationships you have, the richer you become.

The process of becoming a Spiritual Millionaire produces peace of mind. The more peace you have, the richer you become.

The process makes you a generous giver. The more you give, the richer you become.

There are many benefits to becoming a Spiritual Millionaire—and they all deal with who you are becoming.

Who you are *becoming* is always more important than who you *currently* are. It's good to have a strong identity but it's even better to know you are developing an even stronger one. Spiritual Millionaires are always seeking to become more than they currently are. When you become more, you will achieve more.

The Spiritual Millionaire is obsessed with personal development. He is always looking to expand his heart and mind. He sees growing as one of the main purposes of life.

You can go far beyond what you ever thought possible if you make the decision to become a Spiritual Millionaire. A Spiritual Millionaire always goes further than they dreamed possible when they began their journey.

Only God knows who you will ultimately become. Commit your life to God and He will start giving you visions of who He wants you to be and what He wants you to do. Listen to the Spirit of Wisdom to fulfill those visions and God will give you bigger visions. God desires for us to become more than we currently are. The Spirit of Wisdom is always ready to take us to the next level. And there is always another level.

Whoever you are today, it is time for you to become more. Whatever you have done, it is time for you to do more. The Spirit of Wisdom can show you ways to grow and things to do that you never dreamed of. Love her and she will show you.

Chapter Fourteen

A Vision of Abundance

Happy is the man who finds Wisdom and the man who gains understanding. For her proceeds are better than the profits of silver, and her gain better than fine gold. She is more precious than rubies and all the things you may desire cannot compare with her. Long life is in her right hand; in her left hand are riches and honor. Her ways are ways of pleasantness and all her paths are peace.

[Proverbs 3:13-17]

RECENTLY, I WAS walking through the woods, down a mountain in North Carolina. It was a cold day in late January. The trees where completely bare and there were millions of leaves on the ground. I was just walking and enjoying the beauty of God's creation, taking deep breaths and relaxing. Then, all of a sudden, I had an enlightening moment. While I was looking down at the leaves I imagined that they were all dollar bills. It was a fun to think that if all the leaves lying on the ground were dollar bills then there would literally be millions and millions of dollars around me.

Then God took the thought a step further. What if every leaf represented a million dollars? Then there would be billions, perhaps trillions, of dollars here. Then I thought of the beach where I walk when I am home. And I thought, What if every grain of sand was a dollar bill? There would be countless amounts of money on the beach. Then I thought, What if every grain of sand represented a million dollars? There is no way I could fathom how much money that is. Then I thought about the stars in all the galaxies. There are trillions of stars in each galaxy and there are trillions of galaxies. What if each star represented a million dollars and that's how much money there is in the world?

The truth is that there is an abundance of money in the world. No one can begin to understand how much money there is. Can you even begin to understand how much a trillion dollars is? And yet, there are trillions of dollars in the world.

I believe I had this vision to once again confirm that whatever amount of money I strive for is not much when compared to how much there is in the world. There is an abundance of money in the world. The Spiritual Millionaire believes in abundance and experiences it.

Let's look at this vision a little differently. What if every leaf, every grain of sand, every star in every galaxy represented an idea that God could give you to make a million dollars? The Spirit of Wisdom has unlimited ideas of how to make millions of dollars. Whether or not She gives you some of those ideas depends on if you are willing to learn the lessons that She wants to teach you.

Are you willing to commit your life to being a student of the Spirit of Wisdom? Are you willing to commit your life to God? I believe most people would say yes, especially if they thought it would make them financially rich.

God will make you rich financially if you are willing to let the Spirit of Wisdom make you rich spiritually, emotionally, mentally, and physically first. You may say, ""Well, that's what I want anyway. I want to have a personal relationship with God and experience His presence every day. I want to have great relationships with people, especially my family. I want to have peace of mind. I want to have a healthy body. And I want to have an abundance of money."

If you want to have all those things and God wants you to have them as well, then why don't you have them? There could be a number of reasons. I will share two of them with you. These may apply to you and they may not. If they do not and you still aren't experiencing the life you believe you were created for, then ask God to reveal to you the things that are keeping you from all that He has planned for you.

The first reason is that you have not yet learned the lessons God is trying to teach you. In other words, you're not ready yet. The power to become a Spiritual Millionaire is in the *process*. Little by little, step-by-step, slowly but surely, the Spirit of Wisdom prepares you to be able to handle the riches that God wants you to experience. You do not become a Spiritual Millionaire in a day, you become one daily.

The process of life is precious. If you are humble, teachable, and open-minded, you will learn the lessons needed to become successful in every area of life. Only when your heart is ready will God bless you with abundant success.

The second reason is that you are not fully committed to God and being a student of the Spirit of Wisdom. Being committed to God and a student of the Spirit of Wisdom means you are willing to do whatever they ask of you. You must be humble.

I know without a doubt that there are many people who feel anger and unforgiving towards someone. Anger and unforgivingness can keep you from being rich in any area of life. It is impossible to become a Spiritual Millionaire with anger and unforgivingness in your heart. God asks you to forgive. Are you willing to let go of your anger and to forgive? If not, then you are not fully committed to God.

There are people who want money only for selfish reasons. You may say, "I want money so I can use it for the good of others." But if you aren't currently giving, then you have deceived yourself. You can't become a Spiritual Millionaire without becoming a giver. Spiritual Millionaires started giving long before they became millionaires. If you aren't giving, it is proof of your selfishness.

God asks you to give. Are you willing to start giving right now? If not, you aren't fully committed to God. I don't know what God may be asking you personally to do right now but, whatever it is, I believe it is connected to one main thing. I believe it is simply to trust in His love for you and to love others with the same love, patience, kindness, and forgiveness that He has for you. Love is the ultimate reality. It is the source of all true riches. If you really want to become a Spiritual Millionaire you must love God, yourself, and others with your heart. You must let go of all unforgivingness and selfishness. If you have truly committed your life to God, then love flowing to you and through you is the proof. If you really love God, yourself, and others then the Spirit of Wisdom will teach you how to become a Spiritual Millionaire.

Commitment to God is the key to becoming a Spiritual Millionaire. Commitment is not just a one-time act. It is a daily commitment to God that makes you rich in every area of life. If it has been a while since you have prayed and sincerely committed your life to God, why not do it right now, in your own way, and remember to do it every day?

Chapter Fifteen

GOD-GIVEN IDEAS

Happy is the man who finds Wisdom and the man who gains understanding. For her proceeds are better than the profits of silver, and her gain better than fine gold. She is more precious than rubies and all the things you may desire cannot compare with her. Long life is in her right hand; in her left hand are riches and honor. Her ways are ways of pleasantness and all her paths are peace.

[Proverbs 3:13-17]

I DEAS THAT COME from God are big. They are so big that they may seem impossible to you. God-given ideas always stretch one's faith. The Spiritual Millionaire lives by faith. He knows that with God all things are possible. The ideas that God shares to make people rich will require His assistance to bring them to pass. God-given ideas can't come to fruition without God.

It requires faith to make massive amounts of money; faith in God and faith in the ideas that He gives you. If the Spirit of Wisdom gives you an idea to create wealth and you say, "That's impossible," you will never become a Spiritual Millionaire. Ideas that come from God will be bigger than you. They may look impossible but they are not. All things are possible to those who believe.

There are many stories contained in Scriptures where God did extraordinary things with ordinary people. Many of the people thought God made a mistake by picking them. Ideas that you receive from God will often make you feel like God has the wrong person. God has never made a mistake and He is not going to start with you. When God gives you an idea, He intends for you to trust in Him to bring it to pass through you. If you have an idea that seems too big for you, that's a sign that it is a God-given idea.

Have you ever had an idea and didn't do anything with it because of fear or doubt, then later you saw someone else making money from the same idea? That was probably a God-given idea; but you chose to fear and doubt instead of using your faith to act on it. When God gives someone an idea, He intends for the idea to be carried out. If they won't do it, He will find someone else that will. When you get an idea from God you must have absolute faith in God's ability to bring it to pass through you.

Faith is not a response to your ability but to God's. Any God-given idea has the power of God to be fulfilled. A God-given idea would be impossible for you alone, but not WITH God. There are people who have received a God-given idea and have not been able to bring it to pass because they are trying to do it on their own. Don't let that be you. When you get an idea that is BIG, trust in God to use you to make it happen. People who try to fulfill God's ideas without God get frustrated and confused because they can't figure out how to make it happen without His help.

God is always with you. You may not always be aware of the fact, because you have chosen to fear and doubt. Fear and doubt come from looking at possible problems. Faith and hope come from looking to God. Notice I said, "possible problems." Many of the problems people worry about never even occur. There is a popular statement that keeps many people from fulfilling the ideas that God has given them. The statement is: "The only problem with that is ..." This is a negative statement. It is a sign of a person who doesn't have much faith. People who doubt God and themselves are always looking for a problem.

You get what you look for in life. If you are looking for problems, you will always be able to find them. The Spiritual Millionaire looks for possibilities. Problem-focused people are narrow-minded; they have a hard time seeing possibilities. The Spiritual Millionaire knows there is always a way.

All God-given ideas will involve having to overcome something. God doesn't give you ideas that keep you on the same level. God-given ideas are meant to take you to new heights. People without faith and hope see problems as stumbling blocks. The Spiritual Millionaire sees problems as stepping-stones.

The Spirit of Wisdom gives you the ability to see things from a positive point of view. Faith empowers you to see possibilities. Fear causes you to see problems. Remember faith is a choice. You have to choose to believe and trust in God and when you do, your faith expands and gets stronger. God gives big ideas to expand your faith. Spiritual Millionaires have an ever-increasing faith. They become more and more successful because they believe in the God-given ideas they receive.

Chapter Sixteen

ALL THINGS ARE POSSIBLE

Happy is the man who finds Wisdom and the man who gains understanding. For her proceeds are better than the profits of silver, and her gain better than fine gold. She is more precious than rubies and all the things you may desire cannot compare with her. Long life is in her right hand; in her left hand are riches and honor. Her ways are ways of pleasantness and all her paths are peace.

[Proverbs 3:13-17]

I T IS AMAZING what you can accomplish when you believe. Success comes in "cans." I can, I can, I can. Be careful about believing anyone who says you can't do something. Don't let other people put their fears and doubts on you. Decide to believe that all things are possible.

The Spiritual Millionaire does not listen to people who tell him he can't do something. Being told you can't is a primary reason that so many people don't. When you believe you can't, then you won't even try. Here's a story to remind you to believe all things are possible.

There was a young man named George who was a senior at Stanford College in 1933. He didn't have the best grades but he believed that if he scored 100% on his final physics exam he might be able to get a job at the college. He crammed so hard for the test that he showed up ten minutes late for class. He went to the professor's desk, got the test, and sat down to begin.

There were eight problems on the paper plus two on the board. He knew there would be straight grading and he would have to get all ten problems correct in order to earn a 100% on the exam. He worked long and hard and finished the first eight problems. He felt they were all correct. Then he started on the two questions on the board. He tried and tried to solve the first problem but couldn't figure it out. So he went to the next problem, but he couldn't solve it either.

When class was over he was depressed. He would have to settle for an 80% on his exam because of the straight grading. Then, when he was about to hand in his paper, he had an idea. He told the professor that he had been unable to finish a couple of the problems and asked if he could have more time to finish the exam. The professor said, "Sure George, just make sure the test is on my desk by Friday at 4:00 p.m. George was excited. It was only Wednesday afternoon and he would have plenty of time to finish the exam.

He worked hard on the two problems over the next couple of days. He would work on one for a while and when he was not be able to get it, he would work on the other one. Finally he solved one of the problems, but he was still upset because it was Friday afternoon and he had to turn in the exam.

He put his test on the professor's desk and left, knowing he would only receive a 90%. He was upset because he knew someone in the class was going to get 100% and it wasn't going to be him.

Saturday was one of the worst days of his life. He couldn't believe that he wasn't able to solve the last problem. Sunday he was awakened by a knock at his door at 8:30 a.m. Half asleep, he opened the door and was surprised to see his professor. The professor said, "George! George! You have made mathematical history!

George was stunned. "I did?"

The professor said, "Yes, I remember you came in late on exam day and you didn't hear me tell the class not to be too hard on themselves if they missed one or two of the problems because there are always those one or two unsolvable problems that even Einstein couldn't solve. I put two of those problems on the board and you solved one of them!" George was speechless. The professor continued, "George, I have already been in touch with the college and they agreed to offer you a job as my assistant, starting in three weeks when you graduate. It won't pay much, but it might have a future."

Have a future, it did. George eventually became a professor, worked at Stanford for over forty years, and was the U.S. ambassador to foreign countries for higher mathematics. Whenever George told the story he would ask, "Do you think I would have solved that problem if I had been on time for the class and heard the professor say that there are always unsolvable problems? I don't think so."

It is amazing what you can achieve when you believe all things are possible. You can do the impossible when you believe you can. If you hear people say something is impossible, don't believe them. Have faith in God. The Scriptures declare: "Nothing is impossible with God" and "All things are possible to them who believe." Here is one more story that illustrates the power of faith:

There was a physics professor who had been listening to a preacher talk about "possibility thinking." The professor wondered if it would work with his students. He tells the story of meeting with some of the other teachers before classes began. The teachers would ask each other which students they had in their classes that year. A teacher would mention a particular student's name and other teachers would say things like, "Oh boy, is he stupid" or "That kid just doesn't apply himself." In other words, the teachers would start the year with a negative viewpoint on some of their students.

The physics professor decided to try an experiment. In the past, half of all his students failed his course. When he met the students this year, he told them that in the past, 50% of his class always failed—but that he had been reading up on the students in this class and they were all able to grasp the concepts of physics. He was excited that he was finally going to have a class in which everyone passed. The professor didn't change any of the testing or how he graded—and everyone in the class passed! In fact, there was only one student who got a C. The rest of the class earned B's and A's.

Is it possible that your life is a reflection of what others have told you you can or can't do? Is it possible that you have been programmed to experience the life you are living? The answer is yes. Life is often a reflection of the expectation of others. How your life is going depends on whose expectations you are living by.

The Spiritual Millionaire's life is a reflection of God's expectations. Spiritual Millionaires listen to the Spirit of Wisdom.

All things are possible if you only believe. You must forget the lies you have been told and listen to the Spirit of Wisdom tell you what you can do. The first story about George shows that you can do amazing things if you haven't been told you can't, and the story of the physics class shows that you can do amazing things if you have been told you *can*.

Spiritual Millionaires have faith. They are possibility thinkers. Whenever you receive an idea, believe that it is possible no matter how impossible it may seem. Always remember, nothing is impossible with God. The Spirit of Wisdom can make miracles happen through you. Believe that you can become a Spiritual Millionaire and you will. The Spirit of Wisdom will see to it.

Chapter Seventeen

ENTHUSIASM

Happy is the man who finds Wisdom and the man who gains understanding. For her proceeds are better than the profits of silver, and her gain better than fine gold. She is more precious than rubies and all the things you may desire cannot compare with her. Long life is in her right hand; in her left hand are riches and honor. Her ways are ways of pleasantness and all her paths are peace.

[Proverbs 3:13-17]

WHAT IS ENTHUSIASM? Enthusiasm is energy. It is a high level of spiritual energy that drives the Spiritual Millionaire to be successful in every area of life. The more enthusiasm you have, the more power you have to fulfill your purposes. Enthusiasm is the result of staying connected to your source. It is an awareness of the Spirit of Wisdom. It is the difference between success and failure.

What is the source of enthusiasm? One of my mentors told me that the word *enthusiasm* comes from two Greek words, *En* and *Theos*, which mean in God or God within. God is the source of enthusiasm. The Spiritual Millionaire has absolute faith that God is within him or her. To develop enthusiasm in your own life, simply believe that God is within you and focus on it daily. The more aware or conscious you become of the presence of God within you, the more enthusiasm you will have.

The Creator of the universe is a personal God. He lives within His creations. You were created to experience the presence of your Creator on a daily basis. The Spirit of Wisdom is a part of who God is and She desires to make Herself known to you. Those who seek Her, find Her. Those who find Her become rich in every area of life. She is the drive in the life of the Spiritual Millionaire. She is the motivation to succeed in a spiritual way. She is enthusiasm.

Many people do not have much enthusiasm because they do not focus on the fact that the Spirit of Wisdom is within them. Some people don't focus on Her and some people ignore Her completely. Ignoring the Spirit of Wisdom is the reason there is so much poverty in the world. Any country, business, or person that pays attention to the Spirit of Wisdom will prosper.

America is a great nation because our founding fathers paid attention to the Spirit of Wisdom. Whether or not America stays great will depend upon the people of the nation focusing on the Spirit of Wisdom within them.

Ignorance creates poverty. The ultimate ignorance is ignoring the Spirit of Wisdom. Ignorance is the reason people do not live with enthusiasm. Enthusiasm is the result of paying attention to the Spirit of Wisdom on a daily basis. Listening when the Spirit of Wisdom speaks keeps a person excited about the possibilities of the future. Enthusiasm is excitement about life. Enthusiasm is believing that things are going to get better and knowing that you are going to be a part of making them better.

ENTHUSIASM

The energy of enthusiasm is stronger than any other force in the world. It has been said that people do things for one of two reasons: either to gain pleasure or to avoid pain. Enthusiasm is pleasure. It is enjoying the presence of God within you. The pleasure that comes from experiencing God is stronger than any motivation to avoid pain.

Acting only to avoid pain is acting in fear. Acting to enjoy the pleasure of the presence of God is acting in faith. And faith is a greater motivating force than any motivation to avoid pain. The Spirit of Wisdom shows you how to avoid pain by seeking the ultimate pleasure of experiencing God within you. Having God within you is a greater force than anything that can ever rise against you. Acting to gain the pleasure of God's presence is the secret of the Spiritual Millionaire's life.

Enthusiasm is knowing that God will always show you how to think, speak, and act to create and maintain a life of abundance. You can't become a Spiritual Millionaire without enthusiasm. Enthusiasm is the result of living by faith, hope, and love. Experiencing enthusiasm is to feel the presence of God. It is to experience love, peace, and joy at the same time.

Imagine feeling every positive emotion that you have ever experienced at the same time—then multiply it by a million. *That* is true enthusiasm. I have tried to describe it with words but words can't effectively communicate what the presence of God feels like. Spiritual Millionaires love the feeling of God's presence within them and they want others to have the same pleasure.

Enthusiasm is contagious. If you have ever been around someone with a lot of enthusiasm you probably felt an increase in energy and excitement. A Spiritual Millionaire's enthusiasm gives light and hope to all who know him.

Chapter Eighteen

MULTIPLE MENTORS

Happy is the man who finds Wisdom and the man who gains understanding. For her proceeds are better than the profits of silver, and her gain better than fine gold. She is more precious than rubies and all the things you may desire cannot compare with her. Long life is in her right hand; in her left hand are riches and honor. Her ways are ways of pleasantness and all her paths are peace.

[Proverbs 3:13-17]

THERE IS WISDOM in a multitude of counselors. Spiritual Millionaires have multiple mentors for every area of life. Mentors expand your mind by helping you to look at things from different points of view. Think about a ball that is half black and half white. If I held the ball up to you with the black side facing you, you would say that the ball is black. But if I held the ball with the white side facing you, you would say the ball is white. And if I held the ball so that you could see both the black and white, you would know the truth. The same ball from three different points of view looks different.

Great mentors help you see the truth. At the very least, mentors help you see things from their points of view. You must be willing to look at things differently to become a Spiritual Millionaire.

Spiritual Millionaires seek mentors for every area of life because they know that the world is bigger than their own limited experiences. Spiritual mentors teach you about God and your own spirit. Emotional mentors teach you how to have great relationships. Mental mentors teach you how to use your mind.

Physical mentors teach you how to stay healthy. And financial mentors teach you how to make money.

The Spiritual Millionaire has multiple mentors for every area of life because no one knows all the truths about any one area of life, let alone all areas of life. The Spiritual Millionaire has a personal relationship with God but also learns from others who have had different experiences with God.

The Spirit of Wisdom reveals Herself differently to each person. The moment you think that your point of view about God, relationships, mental and physical health, and making money is correct and someone else's is wrong, is the moment you stop growing. A Spiritual Millionaire may have one dominating belief system about God and life but she is open to looking at every area of life through the eyes of others. Good mentors tell you what they believe and let you decide for yourself whether or not to believe it too. They don't make you feel wrong for not believing as they believe.

Have you heard the story of the three blind men trying to describe an elephant? One blind man had a hold of the elephant's leg and said, "It's like a tree." Another one had a hold of the elephant's ear and said, "It's like a big leafy plant." And the third man had a hold of the elephant's trunk and said, "It's like a big snake."

The elephant can represent God, relationships, the power of your mind, physical health, or making money. There is so much to know about every area of life and different people know different truths about each area. That's why you must have multiple mentors for each area of life. How foolish it would be for one of the blind men to say that the other two men were wrong in their descriptions of the elephant.

You need multiple mentors to teach you their points of view about God. You need multiple mentors to teach you their points of view about relationships. You need multiple mentors to teach you how to train and use your mind and multiple mentors to teach you how to take care of your physical body. And you need multiple mentors to teach you how to make money.

Each area of life is huge and it is wise to listen to and learn from people who see things differently than you do. Whatever your spiritual preference, it expands your heart and mind to look at God through another's eyes. The Spirit of Wisdom teaches the Spiritual Millionaire to have an open mind on all subjects, especially God.

The way you see the world is based on your own limited experiences. Seek mentors who have had the experiences and live the life that you want to have. Someone who has been married for fifty years thinks differently than someone who has been divorced three or four times. If you want a great marriage, then find people who have great marriages and learn from them.

If you are stressed and worried, find people who are calm and have peace of mind, and learn from them. If you are overweight and out of shape, find people who are physically fit and healthy, and learn form them. If you are broke and don't know how to make much money, find people who are rich and know how to make a lot of money, and learn from them. Someone who makes $500 a week thinks differently about money than someone who makes $5,000 a week. The one who makes $500 a week would do well to find a mentor who makes $5,000 a week. The Spiritual Millionaire learns from people who have achieved higher levels of success than he has.

The Spiritual Millionaire has virtual and personal mentors. A virtual mentor is someone who has written books, produced audio programs, and gives seminars about their area of expertise. The Spirit of Wisdom will often lead you to a book that you need to read, and the author of the book may become a virtual mentor to you through their other books, products, and seminars.

It is easy to find virtual mentors. There are thousands of people who have dedicated their lives to teaching others about certain areas of life. There are hundreds of books about how to buy real estate, invest in the stock market, and how to start a business, written by people who have already done it. There are hundreds of books written about physical health, the power of the mind, and how to have great relationships. And there are millions of books written about different spiritual views. The Spiritual Millionaire continually reads books on every subject of life.

Personal mentors are people you have a relationship with. Spending time in the presence of a personal mentor is one of the wisest things you can do. Personal mentors get to know you personally and can reach you on a deeper level than virtual mentors.

It is important to have multiple personal mentors and virtual mentors. Only having one person teach you about God or relationships or health or money will keep you from becoming all that you are created to be. It is wonderful when you can find a mentor who is knowledgeable on several areas of life. It is more likely that you will need more than one personal mentor for each area of life. The more personal mentors you can find, the quicker you will achieve your dreams.

The Spiritual Millionaire has multiple personal mentors. A personal mentor is not usually a close friend. They can be, but they are usually people who you look up to and admire the levels of life they experience. When looking for personal mentors, find people who will be honest with you. The problem with trying to have close friends as mentors is that they may hold back from telling you what you really need to hear.

A true mentor tells you what you need to hear, whether you want to hear it or not. Personal mentors can seem to be unmerciful at times. The purpose of having personal mentors is to get you to grow. They do this by telling you the truth. The truth can hurt at times, especially when it is in conflict with your current way of thinking and acting.

Personal mentors help you see your life as it is—not worse than it is and not better than it is. Personal mentors don't let you lie to yourself. They hold you accountable to what you say you are going to do and get on your case when you don't.

If you have multiple personal mentors consider yourself blessed. If you don't have multiple personal mentors then start praying for them to come into your life. Start looking for them. The Spiritual Millionaire spends many years finding personal mentors.

A mentor is a great asset in your life. You can't become as successful without mentors as you can with them. One of the ways to find mentors, is to be one. Whatever you do for others, God will have others do for you. The Spiritual Millionaire is a mentor to others. One of the great benefits of being a mentor is you gain a deeper understanding of the truths that you live by. Every time you share what you believe, you reinforce the truths that make you rich.

People who are truly successful and fulfilled actually enjoy sharing their knowledge with others. They enjoy it because they get to experience the joy and pleasure of their success when they share their knowledge. When you talk with people who are successful, listen for the Spirit of Wisdom to talk to you through them. When you mentor others, let the Spirit of Wisdom speak through your mouth. Mentors are a vessel of the Spirit of Wisdom.

Chapter Nineteen

EVERYDAY LIFE

Happy is the man who finds Wisdom and the man who gains understanding. For her proceeds are better than the profits of silver, and her gain better than fine gold. She is more precious than rubies and all the things you may desire cannot compare with her. Long life is in her right hand; in her left hand are riches and honor. Her ways are ways of pleasantness and all her paths are peace.

[Proverbs 3:13-17]

SUCCESS IN EVERY area of life is not a matter of chance rather it is a matter of habit. Spiritual Millionaires have developed habits that make them successful. In order to achieve success, you must define what success means to you, and then develop the habits necessary to achieve it.

What does success mean to you? Keep in mind that there is success in every area of life: spiritual, emotional, mental, physical, and financial. Once you decide what success means to you in each of these areas, then you can develop the necessary habits.

Some of the habits that will be necessary for you to develop are the things we have already talked about. Training your mind, prayer, meditation, visualizing, affirmations, and learning from mentors must become habits to realize the full benefits. When you take time to train your mind every day, you soon become conditioned for success. When you pray and meditate daily, you will learn to love communicating with your Creator. When you take time every day to visualize, you will be amazed at how quickly you reach your goals. When you use daily affirmations, you will live with faith and enthusiasm. When you learn from a mentor, you will receive the encouragement you need to do what you know you can do.

Habits are formed through discipline. If you don't pay the price of discipline, you will reap the consequences of regret. It has been said that discipline weighs ounces and regret weighs tons. Would you rather carry around ounces or tons?

Discipline is only discipline until it becomes a habit. Once a habit is formed it is no longer hard to do. Habitual success is the lifestyle of Spiritual Millionaires. They are always willing to pay the price of discipline to form habits so they will achieve the successes they want.

What do you want? Are you willing to discipline yourself to achieve it? Discipline is one main part of the Spiritual Millionaire's everyday life. As important as discipline is, there is something else that is far more important. It is gratitude.

The Spiritual Millionaire lives in a state of appreciation. The Spirit of Wisdom blesses people with more when people are thankful with what they have. There is no such thing as success without gratitude. Without a grateful heart, your mind will have no peace and your life will have no meaningful success.

Appreciation is not *a* way of life; it is *the* way of life for a Spiritual Millionaire. Being thankful produces a feeling of love in your heart and peace in your mind. When you are thankful, you are acknowledging your Creator. Being thankful is to attribute your success to God's hand in your life. You can feel God's presence within you when you stop and give thanks for your life.

Thankfulness is true riches. Gratitude is the greatest wealth you can possess. The Spirit of Wisdom always rewards appreciation.

What are you thankful for? This question keeps you focused on what is important to you. Ask yourself this question many times every day, especially in the morning. Spiritual Millionaires start their day by giving thanks in prayer. Starting your day by giving thanks puts you into a great state of mind for the rest of the day. Answering the question, What are you thankful for? forces your mind to think positive thoughts. This is one of the greatest ways to train your mind.

When gratitude becomes a habit in your life, you will experience incredible peace of mind. There is so much peace available to you because there is so much to be thankful for. Be thankful for what God has done, is doing, and will continue to do in your life.

If you made time every day of your life to give thanks and to develop the habits of training your mind, prayer, meditation, visualization, affirmations, and learning from mentors, you would become successful very quickly in every area of life. Once these habits are a part of your daily routine you will watch with excitement as your success starts to expand and continues to expand. These habits are just a few simple things you can do every day to become a Spiritual Millionaire. That's all it takes to become successful—just a few simple things.

There are, however, a few wrong decisions that can keep you from true success and cause you to experience failure. Things like complaining, procrastinating, not exercising, and neglecting your deep desires and your purposes in life can keep you from becoming a Spiritual Millionaire.

Being a Spiritual Millionaire is not just a level in life you arrive at, but a lifestyle you live every day. Any time you develop a belief that you have arrived, you will start to depart. As long as you are living, you will never arrive. There is always a higher level to reach for. Spiritual Millionaires live their lives always looking for the next level. They give thanks every day for where they are and look to where God wants them to go next. The lifestyle of a Spiritual Millionaire is one of continual growth in every area of life.

Become more spiritual, develop deeper relationships, expand your mind, keep your body strong and healthy, and accumulate more and more money. The Spirit of Wisdom will bless you with abundance in every area of life if you listen to her. Follow the Spirit of Wisdom and you will become a Spiritual Millionaire.

To receive a free bonus, and for more information about the author and upcoming live events, please visit our Web site:

keithcameronsmith.com